ANDERSON R̶O̶G̶E̶R̶S̶

PRESENTS

QUOTE, BIND

SELL, REPEAT!

Mastering the art of Property & Casualty Insurance

P&C GURU

VIP INK Publishing Group, Inc.

Atlanta, Georgia

Quote, Bind, Sell, Repeat!

Copyright © 2020

ANDERSON ROGERS & ASSOCIATES, INC.

Editor: ANDERSON ROGERS

ISBN: 978-1-7923-4160-1

Cover designed by SK7

LCCN: 2020940154

Published: 7-15-2020

www.AndersonRogersAssoc.com

VIP INK Publishing Group; Incorporated

I ventured into the insurance industry by accident. I can remember the exact moment it happened. It was 2012 and I recently closed my night club after 12 long years of dealing with everything that came with the nightlife. Bar fights, alcohol liabilities, competition, law enforcement, etc. The money was awesome, but it did come at a price. My days often begun at 3:00 pm and ended at 6:00 am. I loved dealing with people on an everyday basis, but the life had taken its toll on me. I needed a change.

Once the club was permanently closed, I packed my things and headed to Atlanta, Georgia for a new start. I had no idea what the start was going to be but there was no turning back at this point. My mother was living in Atlanta at the time so I figured I would crash in her basement until I found this new career path that was supposed to magically appear.

After a few days, I finally got up early enough to start my job search. I went to the veteran's affairs department to see what jobs were available for veterans. The options were plentiful, but it wasn't going to happen overnight, so I decided to go check out a few night clubs to see if they had any part time work for managers, etc.

As luck would have it, I came across an opportunity where the club was looking for a part time manger for 2 or 3 days a week. I took the job and befriended the club DJ who was from Brooklyn, New York. Ironically, our stories were kind of similar he had just left the housing industry as an inspector and was deejaying part time until he could get back into a successful trade industry. He mentioned a P&C insurance class he had signed up for and suggested I give it a try as well.

My first response was. "Insurance, man I can't stand insurance, that stuff is boring and what is P&C?" He went on to say that he knew of a few insurance agents that were making six figure incomes and a P&C Insurance license was all that was required to start writing business and P&C stood for property & casualty. That sparked my interest so I agreed to sign up for the class, what could it hurt.

Four 10-hour days of P & C insurance information was overwhelming to say the lease. How could anyone learn all of this in this small amount of time, study for the test, take the state exam and expect to pass; it seemed IMPOSSIBLE!

I failed the test on my first try by 4 points. I swore I knew all the answers, but I admit that I did not take studying very seriously the first time. The questions were worded in a manner that you could very well come up with two right answers if you did not take your time to read the questions thoroughly in its entirety.

So, I requested off from work those 3 days and studied my ass off with no distractions. I took 5 to 8 practice exams each day to prepare for the upcoming exam. I was determined not to fail!

The day finally arrived, I got to the test sight early to study my notes one last time before entering the building. Thank God, I passed that time, what a relief!

NOW ON TO SIX FIGURES!

SO, I THOUGHT!

Table of contents

The Process

Independent Agent

Full of energy and motivation, now armed with my Georgia Property & Casualty Insurance license. I was most definitely exhilarated about earning six figures in the next few months. I was doing the math in my head on how to achieve this success. "I could sell 200 to 300 policies a week and if I made sure each policy was valued at $1500 or more that will be $450,000.00 a month." Boy was I naive.

After posting my online resume, I started to receive numerous calls for P&C agent positions. I was amazed at the responses. I remembered our class instructor making a comment about the advantages of having this license. He said, "As long as you have your P&C license you will never go without work and should never be broke". I can safely say that was a true statement. The problems lay in what you're looking for. A job or a career?

I decided to take on a few of these interviews. My very first interview was with an Allstate agent. Working with a popular brand like Allstate would be exciting, I thought to myself. It felt good to have the license but not having the experience did place you at a disadvantage when it came to negotiating pay. Before going to the interview, I did my research on the agencies by checking customer reviews, etc.

The reviews were surprisingly the same for all the agencies for the most part. There was a good amount of good customer reviews but there was also a nice percentage of bad ones too. I remember thinking to myself that all these agents can't be all bad. It must be an explanation for the bad reviews because all the bad reviews were similar but at different agencies. I made a note to ask this question during my interview process.

Here I am a free agent looking to catch a lucrative contract. The one thing I knew was numbers, as a club owner I made thousands of dollars a night and built a great living for myself throughout the years. That time really did come for me when I realized that money wasn't everything. Your happiness and the happiness of others outweighs that temporary feeling that money gives you, any day.

I was operating on savings and I knew that in order to maintain my comfortable lifestyle I needed to earn a minimum of $125,000.00 a year. A job wasn't going to cut it, I needed to have the ability to earn unlimited income. My mind was running 100 mph and I almost forgot that I was sitting in an Allstate office waiting to be interviewed. The agent came out and introduced herself, she was very confident and had this charisma about her. I followed her to her office and saw another young lady sitting there as we entered.

The Allstate agent explained that the lady was her best friend and that she owned her own insurance firm as well, but she was an independent agent. She said that both were going to interview me at the same time, present both their job openings and I could ask any questions and decide after we're done. The Independent agent explained the difference between her firm and her friends.

The Independent had the advantage when it came to offering customers insurance because she could offer the customer more options from several insurance carriers. I quickly realized that the two best friends had this all figured out. If the Allstate agent couldn't find a great rate or policy for a customer, she could always refer that customer to her best friend who has the Independent Agency. This taught me that there's an exponential opportunity to earn money in the insurance industry. Before I left, I asked them about the bad reviews I saw online. In so many words both told me that it's a part of the business and that we can't please everyone.

I went on several more interviews before I gave them my decision; 1 more with another Allstate agent, 3 with State Farm agencies, 1 with Farmers, 1 with Direct Auto, 1 with Nationwide and 1 with American Family. All of them were the same; they wanted to pay me a base pay between $1200 to $1500 a month plus 2%-3% commission on new business. This was not going to get me to $125,000 plus a year. The insurance industry is built of captive and independent agencies and each agency is its own entity. That's why you see names like; "Billy Brown State Farm agent, Rick Brown Agency Allstate Insurance, etc."

Captive agents mainly sell their brands while Independents sell whatever brand they want. Most captive agents don't have the authority to write large commercial policies when most Independent agents offer large commercial products as part of their portfolio.

It was obvious to me that I had to go down the Independent path if I wanted to reach that $125,000.00 a year. The caveat to the independent position that I was offered is there was no base pay. You eat what you kill, you most definitely had to have a hunter's mentality. I called the Independent firm owner and told her I would take the position.

The very next day I go into the office to get appointed as a producer with her list of carrier partners. The process took about 7 to 10 days, once completed I was ready to sell. We had a training class to go over the raters and the different carrier systems. That took about two days and then we were on our own. Go Hunt!

WTF!

You have no idea how bad you suck at sales until you go try to do it without any training. Day one, I type a word doc flyer that says; "Auto Insurance! Call for your free quote today". I took them to every car dealership within 3 miles of my apartment. I did this for weeks, passing out 100 to 200 flyers a day. My damn phone only rung one time, maybe!

Most of the car dealers wanted a quid pro quo. "I send you a customer, you drop me a referral fee." I believe the Georgia law was that you could only give gift cards with a max value of $25 at the time. So, the cash was out of the question and I didn't have extra money to spend on a gift card at the time.

My cousin had just moved to town from Tampa to start a new job. She needed renter's insurance and called me to write the policy. This was during my 1st ten days as an Independent Agent. I just got my first policy! My agency principal called me into the office the next day for a meeting.

She wanted to tell me that I was what they called "a natural, a fast starter". I mean, I only sold 1 policy and that was my cousin's, but I went along for the ride. The Independent went on to show me what great premium policies were. These would earn you the most commission. The homeowners, auto, commercial auto and commercial property, Real Estate Investment properties. A renter's policy will pay you $5 or $10 whereas a Home or Auto will pay you $100, $200, $300 etc.

That was all to the meeting, no more training, no one to teach me how to write a pitch for this damn insurance. I needed to desperately fix my pitch, fix my approach, learn how to choose territory and how to close sales. My savings were crashing to the bottom fast! I put every bit of energy and focus I had into this insurance and it wasn't paying off. I didn't go through that course and wreck my brain studying to pass the State exam to just get a damn job making $18,000.00 to $38,000.00 a year, that was chump change. Something had to give.

AON

After a few weeks of pounding the pavement I was not very close to my goal. At this point it was time to create another game plan. I knew I needed training in order to be efficient and successful at the insurance game. So, I decided to go on a few more interviews and maybe take one of those low paying agent jobs just to get some training and add some much-needed currency to my bank account.

While I was headed to an interview with a State Farm agent my phone rung and it was for an immediate opening at a call center for licensed property & casualty insurance agents. I made an appointment to be interviewed the following day then headed into the State Farm office.

The agent was very seasoned and had been in the game for at least 15 years. Before the interview I had to complete an assessment test. Because of my results, I was asked to come in for this interview. There was one other agent in the office besides the Agency Principal. The ambiance was dark and boring, I could smell the desperation.

I see the weekly quotas written on the dry eraser board and one or two marks notating new policies. The agent led me down the hall to the Agency Principals office. We had a great conversation and I could honestly say that I had a better understanding of the overall P&C insurance business after this interview.

The agency principal explained that insurance is a relationship and volume business and that you had to prolifically plant seeds and continuously water them to see any growth. I understood what he meant by that. My question to him was "Ok and how much will I benefit from planting those seeds"?

He replied, "Well that depends on the situation, if I the agency principal is the one paying to plant those seeds then I recoup the larger percentage of commission and the agent gets the least amount". I totally agreed with this statement, but it was at this moment that I realized I needed to be an agency principal and not someone's agent if I wanted to maximize my earning potential.

This guy offered me $1100.00 a month base plus a 2% commission on new business and nothing on renewals. In addition to that he wanted me to give him 35 to 50 names of people I knew here in Georgia that we could call and quote. I just recently moved here and couldn't give him 15 names if I tried. I told him I would think about it and get back to him because I had a few more interviews already set up.

Well once I got in my car, I did think about it a lot. If I took this position, I would be running on the hamster wheel for my entire insurance career because there was no equity in it for me. It all made sense to me now. The equity piece would be the renewals that you receive from previously written policies, that compounded with new business commissions is the incentive that drives an agent to be successful. The only way to get that is to own your own Agency or Firm or get contracted with a Firm or Agency that's willing to give you points off your renewals in addition to the new business that you've written. I knew then that I was not going to take this job.

The next morning, I drove to the other side of town for my interview at the call center. Thank God it was at 10:00 am, the drive alone took me 2 and a half hours. This would be something I had to do 5 days a week if I took this job. Just crazy, Atlanta traffic would raise anyone's stress level. The one positive was, there's no shortage of work for a licensed P&C agent.

The call center had a contract with AON Affinity a UK based company. This position was to write Professional Liability policies for the Health Industry, mainly Nurses, Nurse Practitioners, Instructors, Counselors, etc. It's also known as E&O or Malpractice insurance depending on the line of business.

All you needed to qualify was an active license and you had to complete 4 weeks of paid training. The position paid $3,000.00 a month and it came with medical and a 401K. This wasn't what I was looking for, but it would provide some stability and I would get some good training in the process. So, I took the offer.

During my first year working with AON I moved from agent to Team lead, to Trainer to Supervisor and was also offered a Project Manager position. I loved the position and working with the team daily. I would train a class of 25 individuals every 3 weeks and out of those 25 at least 21 would make the cut.

Within 9 months I grew our number of agents from 15 to 122. At the end of the year AON made the Forbes list for their PL Insurance lines department. By this time my contract was up for renewal and it was time to talk about money. The hiring manager asked me what kind of salary I was expecting so I gave him a number. He said he could honor it and that the contract would be ready in a few days.

Well the contract did come like he promised but the money was 35% short of my asking price. In short, I turned down the contract but was asked by my immediate supervisor to accept it so that AON would renew the call center contract. I explained to my immediate supervisor that if I sign this contract, I will be updating my resume and it will go active tonight on the job sites and I will be accepting interviews. He replied, "That's fair, I do understand".

Within two days, I did receive a job offer which paid a $3500.00 month draw plus commissions on new business and renewals. I accepted the position and turned in my resignation with AON and the call center the next day. The call center has since lost that AON contract because they couldn't maintain those 122 successful trained agents needed to hit their daily and monthly quotas.

The biggest mistake the call center made was not having a licensed insurance professional in the hiring manager position, because of this the appointed person placed no value on insurance agents and what we did. He also underestimated the job markets high demand for licensed P&C Agents. Which eventually led to their downfall.

AAA

A few days after I submitted my resignation, I started my training with AAA Insurance. This would be my first time getting some real Insurance sales training. The call center was all hot leads where the customer called in or applied online to get policies. At AAA it would be a mixture of cold calls, call ins, mailers, etc. This may sound crazy, but I was really looking forward to learning how to correctly do a cold call and follow up on potential leads.

During the first two weeks, I must have done 300 modules getting to know insurance products from Travelers, Safeco, Progressive, Infinity, AAA, ASI, Metlife & Tapco just to name a few.

The most unique thing about working at AAA was the built-in leads derived from the AAA auto club members. All new agents were sent to the AAA training center in Tampa, Florida for one week.

This is what I was waiting for, I knew deep inside that once I've learned these steps that I would be unstoppable.

The one-week training course gave me tons of insight on how to sell, quote and follow up with potential leads. I took that training and tweaked it to work for me. Some of the steps included in their system was unnecessary and would run customers away in my opinion. I placed myself in the customers shoes and asked myself how would I feel if an insurance agent approached me several times for a quote?

I figured out a way to pre-underwrite all my potential leads during our first conversation. With this information I would have everything I needed to get a great premium and coverage for my potential customer. If I nailed it then my closing ratio would remain in the 90 percentiles. During my first week back, I wrote down several sales pitches and used each one for a week until I saw the best results. One pitch placed me in the

Top 10 agents in the Southeast Region during my first 30 days of writing policies at AAA.

Armed with the magic pitch, I increased my cold call volume to 100 calls a day, mailers to 500 a week and emails to 100 a day. Within the next 30 days my office phone started to ring relentlessly. My new customers were also referring their family and friends and I kept the pedal to the medal. Every day I cold called 100 people, sent out 500 mailers a week and sent 100 emails a day.

Very soon after I started maybe two months. I get an office visit from the V.P. He sat at my desk and we conversed about my background and how natural of a salesman I was. He gave me some pointers on some bigger fish (lines of business) to target in the insurance industry so that I could increase my earning potential. I did take his advice and started to target some commercial auto and property leads but at AAA that was limited too. IT WAS MORE MONEY

OUT THERE! The commercial insurance industry is where the big bucks are made in Property & Casualty. I had only been with AAA for a few months so I focused on their products and selling as much of it as I could.

The biggest caveat to being paid on a Draw system is that if your draw is $3500.00 a month and you made $5000.00 in commission you wouldn't get $8500.00 that month but earn an additional $1500.00. Unlike a base pay plus commission which would have been $3500.00 plus $5000.00 which would have paid you $8500.00. That continued to bug the hell out of me, but I needed this experience, so I rode it out for a year and a half. Once the excitement wore off and I felt that I maximized my potential at AAA I started to look for another opportunity that paid a good base pay and decent commission. I was a seasoned Insurance salesman by this point. Show me the money!

Allstate

During my job search for a competitive contract I was contacted by an Allstate recruiter for a position 12 minutes from my house. I was leaving home every morning at 5:55 am to clock in at 8:30 am, the time I would save on driving alone really sealed it for me before I even went in for the interview. I requested the following Tuesday morning off so that I could go to the Allstate Interview. Well I didn't request it; I told my area supervisor that I was coming in a few hours late because I needed to take care of some business.

When your writing 25 to 35 policies a month consistently, you can pretty much write your own schedule. I reached $68,000.00 my first year at AAA, now in my second year the draw was gone, and it was all new business commission along with %2 or %3 on renewals, somewhere along those lines. At that rate it would have taken me another year to reach my goal of $125,000.00 a year minimum. I didn't want to wait that long. I desperately wanted to get back to my six-figure lifestyle and I was determined to get there.

The Allstate interview went well. It came with a $1200.00 base pay and 6% commission on new business, add in the 15-minute drive and there was no way that I was going to turn this contract down. What really attracted me to the position was that this was a new business or new Allstate franchisee. The principal had no experience in the insurance industry, she held an MBA and her sales experience came from running a car dealership and managing a clothing retailer.

She had three other women in the office, no guys. One was a licensed agent who previously worked at State Farm for a few months. One a CSR and the other was newly licensed and I'm almost certain both were her family members. Once I signed the contract, she mentioned that she had a good friend that owned an Allstate agency and that's who convinced her to start an Insurance Agency.

The agency had only been open for 4 months currently; I think. She showed me her eraser board with the current policy count and went on to explain that she expects each agent to write 10 policies each a month. I looked into her eyes and said, "Really, that's too easy. I can do that in a few days and sometimes in a day"! She replied, "Seriously"? I replied, "Yes, give me a month to get acclimated and I will be writing 30 polices in a bad month".

The other two agents heard this and looked up at me with one question. "How long have you been writing insurance"? I replied, "Not long, it's 2014 now and I started in 2012, I believe". Both shook their heads as if to agree. Before I left, I completed the Allstate appointment paperwork to get that process going. I returned to AAA and put in my 1-week notice. I was very excited to be writing business for the Allstate brand, and I can remember thinking that this is just going to be too easy. Boy was I wrong!

My first day as an Allstate LSP (Licensed Sales Producer) was eye opening. I was no longer working for a corporate giant, now I'm in the small business owner's realm. Here, we really eat what we kill. I watched how the agency owner moved throughout the office; could she handle the stress that comes with this business? Can she sell? Does she understand the importance of the customer experience? She had a confident swagger but was smart enough to listen to someone that knew more about insurance than she did.

All eyes were on the new kid. By this time, I was able to quote and write polices. It felt like I didn't skip a beat, my cell phone continued to ring like it did while I was at AAA and why shouldn't it. While there I was the only agent in the office that had authority to take the one company laptop home. Most all agents stop writing policies after 5:00 pm. Compliance told me that it had something to do with the hours and overtime and some kind of legal bull. I simply told them that I never stop writing policies, if my phone rings at 8:00 pm and that person needs auto insurance. I'm writing the policy, so I need that laptop. I signed a release form and it was all mine, none of the other AAA agents even cared. Sad if you ask me but everyone has their perception of what their job or career should look like. Mine was six figures and rising, no exceptions.

I hadn't been in the office for an hour and had written a homeowners, dwelling, motorcycle and auto policy. This lead was one I was working on for a few weeks while at AAA. I had forgotten about the family because they had just moved to Atlanta from New Jersey and called me to get a few quotes some months back. When I answered my cell, I explained that I was no longer at AAA and was now at Allstate. They said that I was their agent and to go ahead and quote them with Allstate. So, I did and sold all the policies that day. Just like that I wrote 4 polices in 30 minutes.

After that call, it dawned on me that I had put myself in a perfect position by planting those seeds while at AAA. Every mailer and email that I sent out to potential customers had my cell phone on them. I remember signing a Non-compete or Non-solicit agreement, but I wasn't soliciting these customers for Allstate. They were calling me because of the previous work that I put in. So, when the Allstate agency owner created my business cards and marketing materials, I made sure that my cell phone number was on all of it as well.

If it isn't broke don't fix it! I wrote at least 18 to 20 policies that first week. The owner had also implemented an incentive program for new business issued. The more policies you wrote the higher your commission and you would get a bonus if you wrote $50,000.00 in premium during the month. I blew that out of the water every month. My best month was 68 policies and I wrote 32 policies in my worst month. The other two agents averaged 15 policies each a month. How could you live off that?

I really could have written 30% more a month but the cons of being a captive agent had begun to show its ugly head. It made my stomach churn every time I couldn't place a warm lead with Allstate. If I was at AAA I knew I could at least place that lead with 2 or 3 other carriers because AAA was actually setup like a brokerage.

As a captive agent, it was like pissing in the wind. It really sucked! Now in my 5th or 6th month, I started to notice the unhappy customers calling and complaining about their increasing rates, crazy deductibles on their homes and a ton of negative things that customers complain about. Right in the middle of that chaos, I received an email from

Allstate's underwriting team stating that they were cancelling the homeowners policy I wrote because the customer had a catastrophe claim on a dwelling that they owned in New Jersey during that flood some years ago.

Wait! What? So, I called to speak with the underwriter for better clarification. Well according to Allstate guidelines the insureds weren't qualified to have a homeowner's policy because of the CAT claim. I replied, "This customer has their home, auto, dwelling and motorcycle with Allstate and you're willing to lose all of that business because of a CAT claim"? "Do you know how hard I worked to get this business"?

The UW replied, "I'm sorry sir but that's our guidelines". I was livid, I knew that this was all bad for me. At this rate I was going to lose a ton of business. Over the next few months, I had to send at least 35% of my generated leads to the first Independent agency that I worked for because I knew she could write the personal and commercial policies that I couldn't while captive at Allstate.

Almost 2 years had passed, it was November of 2015, four days before Thanksgiving. One of my commercial customers from AAA had referred one of his business partners to me. This gentleman was a well-known businessman here in Atlanta and wanted me to insure 3 or 4 private jets, I don't remember which.

This was it! I knew good and damn well that Allstate wasn't or couldn't cover those jets, at least not at this agency. I took all the information needed to do the quote, called my old boss at the independent firm and she was all smiles. She replied, "I knew you were going to be good; you should have stuck it out with me"! I replied, "Yeah, yeah, you're welcome".

That night I tossed and turned then weighed my options. Should I continue down this path or just start my own agency? The next morning, I called the

Georgia Department of Insurance to find out what steps I needed to take to start my own agency.

I filed for a Corporation, applied for direct appointments with several insurance carriers but they all wanted to see your current book of business. I kept hitting this roadblock until I decided to reach out to the old territory managers from Safeco, Travelers, Infinity, etc. I met while at AAA. They all knew me and could verify the policies I've written while appointed with their companies.

I received a few returned calls and they remembered me and the volume of policies that I wrote on a monthly basis. And just like that, I was on my way to conquer the world with direct appointments and receiving 15% to 22% commission on new business and renewals with bonus incentives. My agency launched in January of 2016, to date my book of business consist of 30% Personal and 70% Commercial business culminating in $7,050,463.00 of written premium.

QUOTE

BIND

SELL

REPEAT!

Mastering the art of Property & Casualty Insurance

The Process

1

Initial conversation

Establish trust – Before a customer gives you their hard-earned money, they will need to trust you. Start off by asking insurance questions, like; How long have you been with your current carrier? How's your driving record? Explain how long a violation stays on their driving record versus an At-Fault accident. Explain to them that insurance carries and insurance score just like you have a credit score. Ask them what's more important, more coverage or a good premium. These type of questions and statements will loosen them up and build their trust in you.

Exude Confidence – Always, always be confident in what you're saying when it comes to insurance. Having no confidence is the silent killer. If you feel that you can't answer a question. Tell them you will get back to them with that answer after you look at all the options. Showing them that you're confident makes them that more confident in you.

Display Competence – This is the perfect opportunity to discuss their coverages. Explain to them what's needed and how everything works, ie. The UM, UIM, Comp, Collision, Med pay, etc. If you're not sure of any of these don't discuss it with your customer. Hopefully this is not the case, if so; you need to study until you understand every little piece.

Establish your target – The easiest way to do this is to ask them how much they are paying monthly for their insurance. The outcome to closing this deal depends on it. All agency principals know that we must pay an MVR fee when we quote a customer, some carriers only charge if we didn't bind that customer. These fees can add up if you're not careful.

If you run the initial soft quote without the MVR's and come up considerably lower than the customer is paying now, then you may have a good chance at closing this deal, but the opposite is also true. This is where those questions you asked earlier come into play. "How's your driving record?"

NOTE: *Never, ever give the customer the soft quote. (the quote that doesn't include the MVR's) This will undo the trust that you are working so hard to build. More times than none this quote will not be the true premium.*

2

Mandated = Leverage

A. Most property & casualty insurance is mandated by the Government. The average adult that you will speak to probably has auto, renters, home, business or motorcycle insurance. All those products require insurance before a person could even use them.

B. Once you learn to pre-underwrite your customers, life will run so much smoother. Asking a few pre-underwriting questions will bring you that much closer to understanding your customer. How long have you had insurance? What insurance company are you with now? What made you want to leave them? So, are you looking for better coverage, lower rate or both?

C. Because the Property & Casualty market is so huge, it could be hard to decide on what carrier you want to work or partner with. If you're a captive agent you're probably going to stick with the meat and potatoes of the P&C industry, "Auto & Home" and some small business.

Independent agents have more options because there is no limit on the amount of insurance carriers they can partner with. This also makes it very hard to choose certain lines in P&C, there's just so much to choose from. My advice would be to write out a game plan to obtain a certain amount of premium so that you can increase your bottom line.

Research all the products both personal and commercial. Find which products works with your team best or what products you would like to sell that will help you reach the highest earning potential.

D. Low Risk, High Reward has gotten a bad rep. Some agents look at it as being lazy. They believe that the only way to market for good leads is to spend thousands of dollars a month on warm call transfers and email generated leads. Most of the time those leads are always shared with 2 or 3 more agencies. Spending $20,000.00 a month on leads and closing anything less than 85% is not acceptable but in most cases the closing ratio is around 20% to 35%. Spending $20,000.00 to earn $7,000.00 is throwing away money in my book.

It makes better sense to me if agencies spent that $20,000.00 on mailers, fliers and hand to hand marketing. All those marketing dollars will go towards designing, printing and mailing cost.

E. Repetition eliminates doubt, the more quotes you do the more experience you gain. Insurance is a funny animal when it comes to experience. You may have fell in love with writing homeowners' policies then out of the blue, one of your customers' needs a commercial policy for a new dump truck business they've just started. You have never written a dump truck policy before. Now you're hoping that you can cover it. This will vary depending on your current agencies carrier partnerships and this goes for both captive and independent agents.

By the time you're done quoting this dump truck policy you would have gained enough experience to encourage you to write more of these type policies. I love writing commercial policies, the commission is worth every moment you spend closing the sale.

Every opportunity you get to quote something new, take as a learning experience. The less doubt you have the more your customers will believe in you. Believe in yourself first!

3

Marketing

Mailers | Post cards - This is one of my favorite types of marketing because stamps cost $0.35; you can design the mailers/post cards yourself with an insurance provided template within your carrier's marketing design platform for free. Order a few thousand copies which will be free or for a small fee per card usually $0.45 to $1.15 depending on the amount you order.

Let's just say you can order 20,000 post card fliers for $9,000.00, $7,000.00 for 20,000 stamps and $4,000.00 for direct mail delivery by the designer or printer. You can eliminate the last cost for direct mail by addressing and mailing postcards from your office. It's also very important to scale the post card leads so that one closed lead pays for the entire marketing campaign cost.

You do this by targeting specific P&C markets like fleet trucker polices, etc. Commission from one of those policies will more than likely cover the entire cost of this $20,000.00 marketing campaign. So, if you get one you broke even or may even earn a profit depending on size of the fleet policy. If you get two then it's a magnificent day.

The same concept can be applied to a quote letter sent by regular mail. Your cost would include the envelops, stamps and printing the letters. I know of some agents that have folding machines attached to lead software that automatically prints every lead for you. Leaving the stamping to you or you can also purchase an account with the post office to send metered mail.

Cold Calls – This is that "Eat the Frog" moment for most agents. It's one of those things that you will have to do in this business, sooner or later. Before creating a cold call list, you must make sure that it has been scrubbed for the "Do Not Disturb or No Soliciting Callers". If they're not on your current scrub list and they ask to be removed from your call list, by law you must remove them. Not doing so can result in some costly penalties.

Finding people to cold call has not been easier than it is now with the current technology. There several tech companies that can assist you with building that list or you can create your own way of compiling names and numbers. I like cold calling businesses because for me the reward is higher, and it gets my adrenalin flowing.

Networking Events – these events can be kind of tricky. You will need to do your research when it comes to the location, time of day, who's the host, who's invited, who can I meet, can I build a fruitful business relationship with the people there?

I have always found the most success when attending Real Estate events, Business mixers, Open house events, attending several local apartment community events, sponsoring local school events with a booth or table on location.

Most importantly, you must remember that we are in a volume business, so relationships matter. Introduce yourself and your vocation while networking. Make sure you have a name badge on along with something showing your business name & logo. The right person will spark the right conversation if they're interested in insurance, you don't have to oversell. Remember that you're here to network and build relationships so make plans to return.

You can also take the opposite route and try to sell a policy to everyone that you see at the networking event. Whatever gets you the best results, that's what you should do?

5 Mandatory Relationships – If you don't have a relationship with someone from each of these professions than you are losing out on some great referrals.

A. Insurance colleague that doesn't work with you or for you. Someone from another agency. Captive agents should have a relationship with a broker or independent agent. Independent agents should have a relationship with a Captive agent. You never know when you may need each other. I have captive agents calling me all the time to place a customer with one of my carriers because their rate increased on the auto but not the home. I will write the car while my colleague keeps the home. Better than losing both policies, right?

B. Real Estate Agents will always need a good insurance agent close by. Every new home will need insurance, you just need to convince a Real Estate Agent to do business with you. This can be tricky for captive agents because you only have one option, so selling the brand will be important. Independent agents have a big advantage because they can get different quotes to help the Real Estate Agent's customer loan numbers come in under or at closing cost.

C. Mortgage Loan Officers who work with large banks, finance companies and independents can refer some great leads. They're not plentiful like your real estate agents so you will need to be crafty when trying to build this relationship. You can find them by attending banking events where several banks are in attendance. There will always be a brochure or flier somewhere with the list of executives on it.

Get that list and start planning but make sure you're prepared once you're face to face.

D. Car salespeople are plentiful, you just need to find one that can sell cars. There are the huge mega lots, the medium size lots and the small lots. The only thing that should matter to you is the relationship and the volume of customers the salesperson sends you each week.

We are not allowed to give out cash for referrals so you will need to give out gift cards, lunch, coffee, doughnuts etc. Most people prefer cash, so that's why it's important to constantly show your face and drop off lunch, coffee, etc. the following day or at least once a week if their sending you a good volume of people.

NOTE: *The key is to have leads coming in from multiple sources.*

E. Customer referrals are like gold. Always ask for a referral after you sell a policy. It's also good practice to ask for a referral even if you couldn't sell the quote.

We always send out referral gift cards to our insureds that send us referrals. Some of the insureds are so proud to receive a gift card for referring people that they make it their mission to do so every month.

We only send referral gift cards if we sold the policy. The choice is yours.

Not rewarding your insureds will kill your customer referral leads. There is a value limit that you can give to a customer for each referral. Check with your Department of Insurance for that number.

4

Popular Products

1. **Auto** – The auto policy is the most popular among the P&C line of products. Every agent should master writing auto policies, the caveat is the low premiums offered for some 6-month policies. As an Independent I prefer to pair my customers with the carriers that offer 12-month auto policies.

15% commission on a 12-month auto policy generates more commission along with stronger retainability for your customer. In order to write good policies, you must be familiar with your carrier appetite. This will save you both time and money. All money isn't good money, i.e. If you quote a customer whose insurance history dictates that they don't pay their bills, have several violations within a 1 to 2-year period, switch insurance carriers every six months or doesn't have any prior insurance. You may want to think twice before binding the policy. If a person shows you who they are, believe them.

Most carriers have triggers in place during the quote process that will populate the needed information for you to make this decision. You should be 100% sure because the last thing you want is a charge back. We're in business to make money not give it away. This can be especially hard for the new agent that's trying to build their book of business. Don't get me wrong there is a market for non-preferred customers and if that's your niche then so be it.

2. **Home** – The homeowner's policy is the next most popular P&C product. The majority of HO3 policies are billed to the mortgagee up front and at renewal, for new business the closing attorney sends out the payment during the home purchase closing. Like any other policy the secret to retaining a homeowner's policy is to give the insured what they ask for and explain what they don't understand.

    Some carriers have 2 or 3 deductibles attached to their HO3 policies. It's a must that you explain this to your insured if you place them with these type companies. The last thing you want is for your customer to file a claim and get hit with a $5000.00 deductible. I can almost guarantee you that they will be shopping for a new carrier after that bad experience. If you give your customer a 1%, 2%, 3%, 4%, etc. deductible, please explain to them how that 2% deductible is calculated. Yes, premium is important but so is coverage. Raising the deductible to get a lower premium without discussing it with your customer will more than likely lead to a charge back or non-renewal not to mention the bad customer service and reviews.

It's very important to know your carrier appetite. Some carriers give insureds a pass for CAT claims and some don't. It's your job to know that. If you quote a home and see a pattern of the same type claims. You may want to find another market to place that customer in, they probably won't qualify for a preferred policy or the premium may be ridiculously high.

There all types of discounts that come with HO3 policies. Alarms, new roof, new home, gated community, electric, plumbing, heating and AC updates. Always try to bundle home and auto when applicable to give your insured the multipolicy discount.

Note: *Insurance is a for profit business. The more claims you have in your book of business the less profitable your book will be. Most Agency principals have an opportunity to earn a profit-sharing check if they keep their loss ratio under a certain number.*

3. **Toys** – RV's, Motorcycles, Jet Skis, ATV's and Boats are considered toys within the insurance industry. Most of the written premium for toys are very low except for boats and RV's. These

products are mostly written during cross sell with the home and or auto. The insured will also receive a multipolicy discount. If you're in an area that has a mass of boats and RV's you should focus on building a book around this market.

4. **R.E.I. Properties** – Building a book focused on real estate investment properties can earn you huge commissions but you will need to put in the work and be partnered with the right carriers. One of my R.E.I. insureds has 52 dwellings in Atlanta, Georgia and his yearly premium is $305,800.00 the carrier that I placed him with pays my agency a 22.5% commission. That's a $68,805.00 commission check that will be deposited every April as long as we do our part and keep the insured happy.

Knowing your carrier appetite will help you target the huge policies. If your carrier doesn't write apartment buildings or R.E.I. properties, then you may want to consider a different carrier if your goal is to make unlimited income.

5. **General Liability** - Slip and fall coverage is most common among business polices both small and large. It usually covers persons injured on your business property when the liability is not caused by you. Artisan contractors such as cleaning services, contractors, plumbers, etc. are required to have general liability before they can conduct business.

   If there is a business office involved the property manager or landlord usually requires to be listed as an Additional insured or a Certificate Holder. The usual required limits are 1 million per occurrence and 2 million aggregate. Your carrier will have an appetite showing which professions they cover.

6. **Commercial Auto** – A few good C.A. polices a month will pull any insurance agency into an entirely new tax bracket. The average insurance agency normally writes personal auto and maybe a few artisan or contractor auto policies but the premium for PL and Artisan lines doesn't compete with trucking, tow truck, dump trucks, fleet, bus policies, etc.

A $1200 PL auto or $5,000.00 artisan auto is chump change compared to a $85,000.00 Trucking for hire policy or $158,000.00 fleet bus policy. Most commercial carriers pay between 10% to 15% commission on their polices on new business and renewal. In my opinion and from my experience, any agency will be doing themselves a disservice if you're not writing any commercial auto business to enhance your PL book of business.

However, you don't want to just write any type of commercial auto business. It's very important that you understand how to write these policies and who to write. Make sure that you are appointed with the most competitive carriers and please, please try your very best to write insureds that have been in business for at least 2 to 3 years.

When my agency first ventured down the commercial auto path, we took on a few new business owners and ended up paying back some healthy commissions because the insureds just couldn't handle the premium. Their lack of experience hindered them from contracting enough business to remain operational. NOT A GOOD SITUATION FOR ANY AGENCY TO BE IN.

It's pertinent that you do your due diligence when hunting C.A. biz. Now I require a minimum of 2 years in business and a prior declaration page for proof of coverage. If they have a DOT number get it and enter it in SAFER WEB government site to research the company before you write the policy.

When determining what lines of commercial auto, you want to hunt, it's important to know what products are needed for their type of business. Some polices require GL (General Liability), Cargo, etc. Make sure your carriers offer all needed products. The last thing you want to do is write a policy then find out later that the customer needs an extra 2 million in cargo coverage, but your carrier doesn't exceed 1.5 million.

This could very well mean that you will lose that customer and be stuck paying back your hard-earned commission. Again, make sure you do your due diligence before entering the commercial auto insurance world. The more quotes you do, the more experienced you become.

7. **Commercial Property** – C.P. can be very tricky depending on both the carrier and product. Most carriers require photos before you can issue a policy. If you're dealing with a busy customer who doesn't have time to take the pictures or just doesn't want to. Well you may have a problem,

especially if they are already insured and you want to win that business.

I recommend you keep someone on call to take pictures when and if needed to avoid that hiccup. There's a wide range of C.P. that you can write. Apartment buildings, shopping malls, warehouses, schools, hospitals, airplane hangars, stadiums, arenas, dwellings, business parks, office buildings, skyscrapers, etc.

Most carriers pay 10% to 22% commission on new business and renewals. Unlike C.A. the C.P. policies can take longer to write depending on the size of the property, photos, inspections, etc. In my experience, many insureds are mostly concerned about coverage and not so much premium.

You really need to have several carriers if you decide to write any C.P. business. Some buildings may be old with copper pipes, fuse boxes instead of circuit breakers, cracked parking lots, etc. Which will all be denied by the average underwriter. The last thing you want to do is spend several hours quoting a commercial building and have the quote denied.

Find carriers that will write class A, B and C properties and get familiar with each one so that you can pre underwrite your customers. We're in business to make money and underwrites are in business to prevent insurance companies from paying out as much as possible. So, if they see a potential risk, they will deny your quote, make no mistake about it.

One of my first C.P. customers is in Michigan and he has 5 dwellings throughout the city. I placed his properties with a carrier whom I won't mention and received a healthy commission. Well 60 days later after the inspections, some of the buildings were deemed unfit due to a roof and piping. They didn't require photos during the quote process which would have saved me time and money.

The company cancelled 2 of the policies and I had to move them to another company. My customer however wanted to keep all the properties under the same company, so I had to requote all the properties again but with a new carrier. This was one of those times that I was happy to be an Independent agency appointed with several carriers. Yes, I had to do more work, but I kept the customer. The moral of the story; make sure you have several options and know the pros and cons of each. The 1st carrier paid 12% commission but the 2nd carrier that I moved all the dwellings to, paid 18% commission on a $475,000.00 premium. I LOVE THE INSURANCE BUSINESS.

5

Insurance Carriers

1. **Captive** – In my opinion most of the pros of being a captive agent is because of brand recognition. There's not a day that goes by that you won't hear or see advertisements about an Allstate, State Farm, Geico or Farmers, etc. Many people feel more secure when their products are insured by a popular brand.

   This makes it somewhat easier for captive agents to sell the brand to potential customers. Attaching yourself to a popular insurance carrier is great marketing. You really must know the carrier's appetite in order to capitalize on the brand. There will be several instances where you'll find yourself selling a carrier's brand and their ability to pay claims over the policy premium. I've had the opportunity to work for a captive agency after I've been exposed to the non-captive side and boy is it a difference.

Several cons come with being a captive agent. The most obvious is you have less options to offer your clients. If the premium is too high and your customer wants to switch to a different carrier. Well, you just lost that customer if you can't find a way to lower their premium.

The average captive carrier pays a commission of 6% to 10% per policy for new business. If you work for a captive agent there's a good chance that you will average under $35,000.00 a year. The industry standard for pay structure is a base pay plus 2% to 3% commission on new business and %0 on renewals. This structure doesn't offer you a residual piece of the book of business which means you will always be in the rat race with no opportunity to grow financially.

As a captive agent you will find yourself turning away a lot of business because you are not equipped to write it. Sometimes you will end up losing or referring your insureds to industry colleagues because of increased premiums at renewal.

2. **Independent** – If you entered the insurance industry to make money then the sky is the limit when you're an independent agent. What you earn really depends on the direction that you want to go in. You can choose to write high end commercial policies or standard auto and home policies, etc.

There's plenty of insurance carriers that you can write business with and you can choose as many as you like. You can build your book of business to fit any market while earning six figures or more a year or even in a month if you want to.

The average independent carrier pays 10% to 22% commission on new business and renewals. In addition to the commission you can earn profit sharing checks, quarterly bonuses and cash in on monthly contest. You will be invited to industry events on a regular and you get to meet your territory managers every other month to discuss business while enjoying breakfast, lunch or dinner on the insurance carriers' dime.

As an independent, each carrier that you're appointed with, normally will require a monthly commitment from you or your agency of 2 to 5 policies a month, exceeding those numbers usually comes with some great incentives. As an Agency Principal I always share those incentives and or profit-sharing checks with my hard-working agents.

This is my decision and not industry standard, I know of some fellow agency owners that keep everything to themselves. I just believe in teamwork and rewarding the team for a job well done. Profit sharing checks are earned when you meet or exceed a predetermined premium within a set period and maintain a low loss or claims ratio. Not all carriers offer profit sharing checks so when searching for carriers to represent be sure to ask the question, if you want to be involved in such opportunities.

It must be one of the best feelings in the world when you can move an unhappy customer from one carrier to another within your firm when their current premium increased at renewal with their current carrier. You end up keeping the customer and not losing any equity because of it. YOU CAN'T DO THAT AS A CAPTIVE AGENT.

I will admit that starting your own Independent agency will be hard in the beginning because most of the carriers aren't looking to appoint inexperienced agencies. It becomes tricky at this point. There several MGA's or Wholesale Agencies in the industry that will appoint you to write business under their firm for 30% to 40% of your commissions on new business and renewals. Most of the time it's extremely hard to get out of these contracts without losing. Some require that you wait at least 2 years before getting a direct appointment with a carrier that they represented.

This is a bilateral contract and the same rules apply to the carrier as well, so you will have territory managers ask you if you're appointed with any MGA's before they give you a direct appointment. My advice is to find the best fit for you and please, please, read your contracts thoroughly.

30% to 40% is a large chunk of equity to be giving away when you have monthly overhead to pay as well before you pay yourself. So, think long and hard about that. I was lucky because I knew several territory managers from my time at AAA and I wrote a lot of business for them during that time, so getting a direct appointment was easy.

I pay my agents a competitive commission on new business and renewals and we give them free leads every week to help build their book of business. This way every agent will have equity in the firm. There's no better feeling than having new business commissions on top of renewal commissions when pay day comes. It makes all the effort and hard work that much sweeter.

3. **Carriers with best commissions –** Nationwide, Universal, Travelers, Berkshire Hathaway are some of the few that pay a great commission percentage on new business and renewals. Berkshire however pays on an as earned basis. This means you will get paid your commission on a monthly basis whenever your customer pays their premium. Most insurance carriers pay the

full commission percentage the following month or within the next 30 days.

Most of these carriers do require that you have at least a minimum $4,000,000.00 book of business before they will appoint you. They will want to see copies of your monthly production or year to date production numbers along with quotes and closing ratio. This is the caveat that leads many aspiring agency owners to join MGA's and give away a big chunk of their livelihood.

4. **Building a Book of Business** - Because of the vast size of the insurance industry this can be a bit overwhelming. I would recommend a few important factors to remember when deciding what customer markets to target when building your book. 1) Look at your current customer base and determine

where you favor better. 2) Research your city, neighborhood and population. 3) What commercial business markets are popular in your city or town? 4) What's your close ratio? 5) Can your agents write policy? 6) How much competition is there in your area? 6) What makes you different from your competitors? Focus on that! 7) Decide on the premiums and markets you would like to target. 8) What's your marketing budget? 9) How are you going to attract those customers?

Most important! Know what products your appointed carriers offer and how it can affect your bottom line. 10% on renewals vs 15% on renewals can make a large difference in profits. If you're not satisfied with your current options, seek out the carriers that offer the products that you want to sell. Of course, the options will be limited for captive agents but for independent agents, the world is your oyster.

6

Renewals

1. For the professional insurance salesman, having a commission from your renewals is like Heaven on earth. It makes your hard work and effort worth it. Yet, most agency owners only pay their agents a base pay plus a small commission on new business. If you're only looking for a job than this maybe ideal for you but if you're looking for a career and a comfortable life than I suggest you start your own firm or find a situation that will pay you on both New business and renewals.

   Having equity is the key to success within the insurance industry. If there's no equity you will find yourself earning $18,000.00 to $35,000.00 a year and moving from agency to agency.

Any agent worth their salt can earn that in a month if they have the right products to sell in addition to renewal commissions on your previously written policies.

There's always the argument of "I paid for the leads so I as the agency owner deserve 100% commission on all renewals". The one thing I can tell you as an Agency owner is that everything can be negotiated when it comes to how we pay agents. The agent just hardly ever tries to negotiate. If you as an agent know that you can sell any policy and your close ratio is above average. Try telling that agency owner that you will give up the base pay for a percentage of the renewals. Most of the time they will say, Absolutely!

Most P&C agents obtained their insurance license so that they can earn great money. $35,000.00 a year is not great money. $60,000.00 is only ok money. Don't settle for what the industry offers, you can earn any amount you want when you know how to get it. Selling only home and auto insurance can get you to six figures a year, if you're in the right contract and willing to do the work.

Decide what you want to earn, how you're going to get there then start taking the steps to make it happen. In P&C, the largest premiums will always be in the Commercial Auto & Commercial Property markets.

7

The Quote

1. **The quote** – (Get all needed info during the initial conversation and always utilize your resources)

(Cold call)

AGENT: Hello Ms. X

LEAD: Hello!

AGENT: My name is Agent with ABC Insurance and I'm calling to see how I can save you some money today.

LEAD: Oh really!

AGENT: Yes, how much are you currently paying a month for your auto insurance? Did it go up within the past few months? (*this is establishing your target*)

LEAD: Why yes it did! I'm paying $350.00 a month.

AGENT: And that's why I'm calling. Can you confirm your address for me?

LEAD: It's 123 Lovers lane, Atlanta, GA. 30345

AGENT: Awesome, the number that I'm calling, is it a good contact number?

LEAD: Yes, it is.

AGENT: And to make sure that I have your name spelled right. Can you spell it out for me because any mistakes can cause your auto quote to increase and we don't want that!

LEAD: Sure, it's....

AGENT: Thank you and what's your birthday young lady?

LEAD: It's 12/05/1975

AGENT: Great, just a few more questions and I can get started on saving you some money. Maybe you can use it to treat yourself to a spa day or something. (*establishing hope*)

LEAD: That would be nice.

AGENT: What's your driver license number and a good email address for you?

LEAD: It's 050222999 and my email is my first name dot last name at gmail.com.

AGENT: Awesome, so what insurance company are you currently with and how long have you been with them? (*pre-underwriting*)

LEAD: I'm with EFG and I have been with them for at least 3 years now.

AGENT: That's good and how's your driving record? Do you consider yourself a good driver?

LEAD: It's ok, I have a speeding ticket.

AGENT: When did you receive that ticket? (*pre-underwriting*)

LEAD: It's about 2 and a half years old.

AGENT: That's great because it only stays on your driving record for 3 years so it shouldn't affect this new quote too much. (*educating the customer*)

LEAD: Thank God!

AGENT: I know right and tell me; Ms. X, how many cars do you have on your current policy? Do you have full coverage or just liability?

LEAD: I have two cars; the newer one is full coverage and the other one liability only.

AGENT: Awesome, I will need those VIN's. You can read them to me, or you can take a pic of them with your cell and text them to my business cell. Whichever is easier for you.

NOTE: For commercial quotes this is where you ask for the declarations page. Have them email it or fax it to you. In some cases, you may proceed without it but in my experience it's always best to have it. More times than none the customer usually doesn't understand their coverages or what's required based upon the risk.

LEAD: Ok, I can read them to you.

AGENT: Thank you and what day of the month do you make your current insurance payment; do you want to keep your new policy payments on the same date? (*start closing the sale*)

LEAD: The 15th but if you could set it to the 20th that would be so much better!

AGENT: No problem, I can do that. (*establishing trust*)

LEAD: Thank you!

AGENT: Ms. X, I'm going to need about 10 to 15 minutes to run some quotes for you. I want to make sure that I'm doing all that I can to save you some money. I have everything I need to acquire some quotes, so you can go relax and I will be contacting you in a few minutes. If you don't answer your phone, I will text and/or email the quotes to you.

(*I never keep my customers on the phone while I'm quoting. It slows me down but it's totally up to you. There is no need to worry about losing them if you followed the above steps. You don't want to seem overly aggressive.*)

LEAD: Ok and thank you.

After you have secured a great quote

(*Scenario 1: You call, customer answers*)

AGENT: Hey, Ms. X

LEAD: Hey, do you have good news?

AGENT: Yes Ma'am! I can get you in at $285.00 a month and I set your future payments up for the 20th.

LEAD: That is wonderful, will I have to pay it now?

AGENT: Well today is the 13th so why don't you make the payment on the 15th. So instead of paying $350.00 to EFG on the 15th you can pay $285.00 for your new policy on the 15th. You can treat yourself to that spa day with the money you saved. (*cementing the sale, assuring her that she can spend that extra $65.00. She will make a mental note and will call you on the 15th if you don't call her 1st.*)

LEAD: Ok that works for me and thank you so much.

AGENT: My pleasure, I will speak with you in a few days.

(Scenario 2: Customer doesn't answer)

Agent leaves voicemail, email and text consisting of the following message.

Hi, Ms. X it was a pleasure speaking with you today. I found a great rate for you. The monthly payment will be $285.00, and I also secured your recurring payment date for the 20th of the month. So please contact me as soon as you can. I don't know how long I can guarantee this rate. Have a great day!

NOTE: *I never send the customer a copy of the quote unless they ask for it. A lot of customers like to shop around and pass your quote to a different agent to see if they can beat it. I only send the premium; I don't even send the name of the carrier because as their agent. I want them to trust me and that my word is gold.*

Follow up to bind policy

Set a reminder on both your phone & pc calendar to do a follow up call a day or so before you want to bind policy. If you're disciplined enough the calendar will act as your secretary. JUST DON'T IGNORE IT!

Closing notes

Coming in under target almost always guarantees the sale. If for some reason you can't come in under target. Sell the coverage and/or yourself, your professionalism has value and sell the carrier's brand. People love to be associated with great brands.

If you're a broker and can offer your customers several options. Always choose the carrier with the middle premium if you come in under target. By doing this you secure more options for the customer in the future if the policy you're writing for them now increases at renewal. If you give them lowest option, where are you going to put them if that policy increases at renewal? After all, you're still saving them money.

All great insurance agents know to secure the account and not focus on a policy. If the customer has a home, insure it. A boat, insure it! A motorcycle, insure it! A business, insure it! RV, insure it! Jet ski, insure it! An investment home, insure it! You get the point, right. Write the account and not just a policy.

Agents should always ask for a referral after speaking with an insured. The same goes for customers that you couldn't insure, always ask for a referral. It's the key to making this insurance thing work. Referrals! Referrals! Referrals!

Leads

Leads are all around us, a P&C agent could never run out of leads. Most of us don't know how to check our ego, that's the problem. P&C Insurance is mandated by the Government so everywhere you look there's an insured. Just think about it. There are hundreds of ways to approach people, just find what works for you and go for it. If you want to spend $5,000.00 a month buying shared leads, it's your money do that. If you want to attend several networking mixers a month, do that. Just don't say there isn't any leads, that's just your excuse.

How to create a lead for free.

Scenario: Store parking lot, you're walking into the store and see a person getting out of their car, maybe it's a nice car, maybe it's a new car with paper tags or maybe it's just a regular car. Taylor conversation accordingly.

Agent: Excuse me sir! That's a really nice car! I was thinking about getting one, how does it drive? (*cater to their ego*)

Lead: Thanks man! Oh, I love it!

Agent: I bet! How much is the insurance costing you on that? If you don't mind me asking. (*shows more interest*)

Lead: Now that's a different story, it's costing me $455.00 a month with EFG company.

Agent: Really! That's interesting because one of my customers has one and it's only costing him $295.00 a month but he's not with EFG. (*empathy and establishing another competitor*)

Lead: What! Are you kidding?

Agent: No, I'm serious. Oh, my name is Mark by the way and yours? (*building relationship*)

Lead: It's Daniel, nice to meet you Mark.

Agent: Nice to meet you Daniel, if you want; I can give you my number and I can see about getting you a lower rate like my customer has. We can all stand to save a few bucks, right? (*locking in lead and show's you want to save him money*)

Lead: That would be great Mark, what's your number?

Agent: It's 404-888-9999, oh text me real quick so I can lock in your number and I'll know it's you when you call. (*Confirming interest*)

Lead: There you go, did you get it?

Agent: Yep, got it. So, give me a day or so before you contact me or I'll just text you once I'm free and we can see what kind of rates I can get for you. Doesn't hurt to try, right? (*creating fear of lost, he'll be waiting on your call and doesn't makes you appear to be eager which is always a bad sign*)

Lead: Thanks, Mark.

Agent: You're welcome Daniel, I better get going before my wife starts calling and asking what's taking so long. (*further cementing relationship and showing that you're human*)

Lead: Yeah, me too! Talk to you soon Mark. Have a good evening.

Agent: You too man! (*you just made a new friend and customer. If this goes right, he'll refer all his friends and family members because of your relationship*)

(*Once customer leaves put his info on your phone calendar and set it to go off a day or two from that date. Make a note:* "**Daniel, luxury car lead from store parking lot. Call to start quote, currently paying $455.00 a month with EFG.**")

NOTE: *Remember! Go for the account not just the policy!*

Go that extra mile.

Business is both War and Sport, take this next case for instance. A referral called me and asked for an auto quote because they were tired of getting ripped off by their current carrier and said that their agent was an asshole. Their sister is insured by our firm and she recommended that they give me a call.

So, I got all the needed information and asked the customer to send me their declarations page because I really wanted to see how the agent had written the policy and what agency it was.

Once I received the dec page I saw that it was a captive carrier and I knew right then that I could beat the current premium but wasn't sure of the customers insurance score, so I matched the coverages and ran the MVR.

Their score was not that good, so the carrier I quoted them with required a higher deposit. The customers current policy was set to renew 30 days from the day they called, so it gave them some time to come up with the down payment.

I had no idea what that agent had done to this customer, but the family was adamant about leaving them. They were not happy about the double down payment and asked if I could do something about it. I said sure but listen closely and you will need to follow my instructions step by step.

Since the policy was not going to renew until 30 days from now, I did a bare bones quote and removed all the coverages from the policy except for liability. That in turn dropped the premium and down payment so that the customer could afford to make the initial payment, but it had to be done before their current policy renewed.

I explained this and the customer said that they could make the initial payment that day. Once I took the payment to bind the policy I told the customer to wait the next day before they cancelled the other policy because I needed to add full coverage to their new policy and that once I added this coverage the new insurance carrier would divide the new endorsements evenly over the next 11 months.

The final premium was $75.00 a month less than their old premium. I then created a cancellation request form so that the insured could send it to their old carrier the next day, after I have added full coverage back to their policy. I also explained that they could not cancel their old insurance policy until after 12 noon the next day because I needed to endorse the new one the next morning. The insured obliged and sent the new declarations page along with the cancellation request to their prior carrier after 12 noon the next day. They went on and on thanking me for getting them away from an unhappy situation.

I gained a new customer and the prior agency lost a paying customer and gained a charge back because the policy had been canceled prior to its renewal.

This scenario is not applicable with all carriers, some carriers will require an additional payment on the day of any new endorsements.

ABC (Always Be Closing)

Always give your customers your business cell number. This isn't a 9 to 5! Put yourself in a situation where you're always available to write business. Referrals come at all hours.

Most of the agencies in our industry are closed between 5 to 6 pm Monday through Friday and some do not even open on Saturday and Sunday. You will be surprised at how much business you'll end up writing if you make yourself available after business hours. I wrote 60% of my business after hours during my first 2 years as an agent.

This last year I have been traveling around the country going to different agencies teaching their newly licensed P&C agents how to sell property & casualty insurance. I promise you that every agency I visited closed at 5:00 pm or 6:00 pm Monday through Friday.

Most of the agents I've trained increased their sales by 30% to 40% or more and a lot of it is because I helped them tweak their pitch and they made themselves available after normal business hours. If you want to make a career out of this, you can't think and operate like a 9 to fiver!

The only way to obtain the quality of life that you seek is to step your game up! Whenever I get tired of working here in my city, I book a flight to South America, Jamaica, Cancun, California or even Florida. I'll book a room or AirBnB on the beach pull out my laptop and get some work in during normal business hours then go grab a Mai Tai and some seafood after 5 leaving my business cell on until 9. I call it WorkCation.

Sitting on the beach without a care in the world knowing that you have compound income coming in every month. That is the ultimate goal, it's why we all do this, right. If not, then what's the point?

I built a 7-million-dollar book of business in 4 years; my agency has hundreds of agents across several states and we're steadily growing. Another agency owner once told one of my agents that P&C agents could only average around $37,000.00 a year. I laughed at her and told her, I was told that too, but I make that in a month. Don't believe everything you hear; I'm living proof and I can show you how to make $37,000.00 in a month too.

Write your own check!

I always keep track of my daily sales by inserting them into a monthly excel spread sheet. Set a goal for the week and track it as you go. Label your first excel row as follows:

Insured | L.O.B. | Item count | Premium |Effective date | End date | Policy # | Bound date | Notes |

You will be able to calculate the premium column to track your goals.

www.AndersonRogersAssoc.com